Ecosystems
Chaparrals

Michael de Medeiros

www.av2books.com

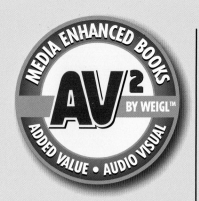

AV² provides enriched content that supplements and complements this book. Weigl's AV² books strive to create inspired learning and engage young minds in a total learning experience.

Your AV² Media Enhanced books come alive with...

Audio
Listen to sections of the book read aloud.

Key Words
Study vocabulary, and complete a matching word activity.

Video
Watch informative video clips.

Quizzes
Test your knowledge.

Go to **www.av2books.com**, and enter this book's unique code.

Embedded Weblinks
Gain additional information for research.

Slide Show
View images and captions, and prepare a presentation.

BOOK CODE

E 5 0 6 7 4 4

AV² **by Weigl** brings you media enhanced books that support active learning.

Try This!
Complete activities and hands-on experiments.

... and much, much more!

Published by AV² by Weigl
350 5th Avenue, 59th Floor
New York, NY 10118
Website: www.av2books.com   www.weigl.com

Library of Congress Cataloging-in-Publication Data

De Medeiros, Michael.
 Chaparrals / Michael de Medeiros.
   p. cm. -- (Ecosystems)
 Includes index.
 ISBN 978-1-61913-070-8 (hard cover : alk. paper) -- ISBN 978-1-61913-233-7 (soft cover : alk. paper)
1. Chaparral ecology--Juvenile literature. I. Title.
 QH541.5.C5D46 2013
 577.3'8--dc23
                  2011045201

Printed in the United States of America in North Mankato, Minnesota
1 2 3 4 5 6 7 8 9 16 15 14 13 12

012012
WEP060112

Project Coordinator Aaron Carr
Design Sonja Vogel

Every reasonable effort has been made to trace ownership and to obtain permission to reprint copyright material. The publishers would be pleased to have any errors or omissions brought to their attention so that they may be corrected in subsequent printings.

Photo Credits
Weigl acknowledges Getty Images as its primary photo supplier for this title.

Contents

What is a Chaparral Ecosystem?

Most of coastal and inland California is made up of chaparral ecosystems.

E arth is home to millions of different **organisms**, all of which have specific survival needs. These organisms rely on their environment, or the place where they live, for their survival. All plants and animals have relationships with their environment. They interact with the environment itself, as well as the other plants and animals within the environment. These interactions create an **ecosystem**.

Chaparral ecosystems are found in many parts of the world. The word *chaparral* comes from a Spanish word that means "scrub oak." The ecosystem is best known for its dense growth of shrubs and its very hot, dry summers. This heat is a major reason that, every 40 years or so, huge fires destroy large amounts of chaparral.

Home in the Chaparral

Many plants, animals, insects, and other organisms make their home in the chaparral. This makes it one of the most interesting places on Earth to study. Many scientists study chaparral ecosystems.

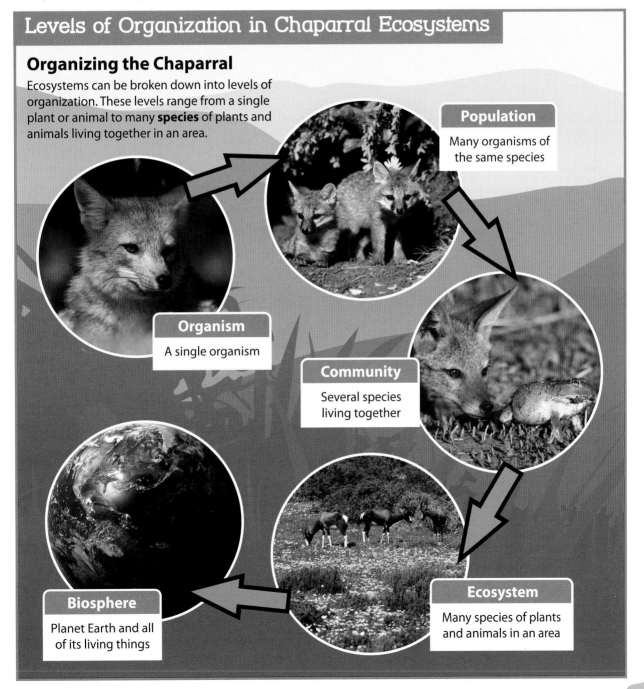

Levels of Organization in Chaparral Ecosystems

Organizing the Chaparral

Ecosystems can be broken down into levels of organization. These levels range from a single plant or animal to many **species** of plants and animals living together in an area.

Population

Many organisms of the same species

Organism

A single organism

Community

Several species living together

Ecosystem

Many species of plants and animals in an area

Biosphere

Planet Earth and all of its living things

Where in the World?

Chaparral ecosystems are often located near mountain regions and along coastlines.

Five of Earth's seven continents have chaparral ecosystems. Chaparral ecosystems can be found in North and South America, Australia, Africa, and Europe. They are found in the southwestern coast of the United States, the western and southern parts of Australia, the coast of the Mediterranean Sea, the Cape Town region in South Africa, and the western Chilean coast of South America. Each of these regions is different. Some chaparrals are on hilly areas covered in rocks, others are in flat, earthy areas, and some are in mountainous regions.

Where to Find Chaparrals

Chaparral ecosystems are only found in areas between 30° and 40° latitude. They are almost always on the western side of a continent. On the western side of continents, the ocean supplies the ecosystem with cooler air and moisture during winter months.

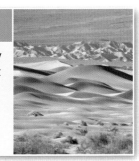

Eco Facts

Chaparral ecosystems are usually found between desert and forest areas or between desert and grassland areas.

Chaparrals make up the smallest **biome** on Earth.

Two chaparral areas that have been studied extensively are the Mediterranean and California chaparral ecosystems. The Mediterranean chaparral includes a large area of land reaching parts of North Africa and Europe.

The California Chaparral

The California chaparral is located on the coast of the southwestern state of California in the United States. It extends into nearby areas, including the Sierra Nevada mountain range. The California chaparral includes mountains and flat lands, making it one of the most interesting areas in the world to study. The fact that the California chaparral is so large and varied means that a great number of different animals, plants, insects, and other organisms make their home in the area. Unfortunately, much of the California chaparral ecosystem has disappeared because of the expanding human population.

❚ Joshua trees are one of the few tree species that grow in chaparral ecosystems. **❚**

Chaparral ecosystems are found on most of the world's continents. This map shows where the world's major chaparrals are located. Find the place where you live on the map. Do you live close to a chaparral ecosystem? If not, which chaparrals are closest to you?

Legend

- ▣ Chaparral
- ☐ Ocean
- ∿ River

Scale at Equator

0   1,000   2,000   3,000 miles

0   1,000   2,000   3,000 kilometers

N

California Chaparral

Location: North America (United States)
Size: 46,800 square miles
(121,211 square kilometers)
Fact: Areas of chaparral ecosystem cover much of California's western coast. These areas can be divided into three distinct ecosystems—coastal scrub chaparral, interior chaparral, and montane chaparral. California's coastal scrub chaparral has adapted to survive the regular fires that occur in the ecosystem. Some of the plants that grow here have seeds that only germinate after a fire. The montane chaparral ecosystems contain peaks up to 11,550 feet (3,500 meters) above sea level.

NORTH AMERICA

ATLANTIC OCEAN

EQUATOR

PACIFIC OCEAN

SOUTH AMERICA

Chilean Chaparral

Location: South America (Chile)
Elevation: 57,500 square miles (149,000 sq. km)
Fact: This ecosystem is known locally as matorral, which comes from *mata*, the Spanish word for shrub. Like its northern counterpart in California, the Chilean chaparral is located in a 62-mile (100-km) wide strip along the western coast. Up to 95 percent of the nearly 1,500 plant species that live in this ecosystem are not found anywhere else in the world.

SOUTHERN OCEAN

ARCTIC OCEAN

EUROPE

AFRICA

Mediterranean Chaparral

Location: Europe, North Africa, Asia Minor
Size: 874,740 square miles (2,265,581 sq. km)
Fact: This ecosystem is home to more than 25,000 species of plants, more than half of which can only be found in this area. The vegetation in this area consists mainly of broad-leafed evergreen shrubs and small trees. Animals that make their home here include leopards, Maghreb deer, the macaque, the Spanish ibex, goats, sheep, and many species of bird. Locally, this scrubland area is called the maquis.

Australian Chaparral

Location: Australia (southwest Australia)
Size: 190,000 square miles (493,000 sq. km)
Fact: One of only five chaparral ecosystems in the world, the Australian chaparral has nearly 3,000 different plant species. Almost 80 percent of the plant species in this ecosystem are not found anywhere else in the world. One of the plant species only found in the Australian chaparral is a type of brightly colored shrub called the banksia.

AUSTRALIA

African Chaparral

Location: Africa (South Africa)
Size: 30,300 square miles (78,475 sq. km)
Fact: The chaparral ecosystem in Africa, called fynbos, is one of the most diverse areas on Earth. Located along the southwestern coast of Africa, this small ecosystem only covers about 0.3 percent of Africa's total land mass. Despite its small size, the fynbos is home to more than 8,500 plant species. In total, more than 5,800 of these plant species are **endemic** to the African fynbos.

SOUTHERN OCEAN

ANTARCTICA

Chaparral Climates

The African fynbos, found along the southwestern coast of Africa, receives moisture from fog that forms over the Atlantic and Southern Oceans.

The chaparral ecosystem has four distinct seasons and is characterized by dry summers and wet winters. During winter, the climate is very mild and moist. Although chaparrals are one of the driest areas in the world, they do receive some precipitation. This precipitation, which is usually between 10 and 17 inches (25 and 42 centimeters) for a whole year, falls mostly during the winter season. For the rest of the year, this ecosystem is hot and dry, reaching temperatures of 100 °Fahrenheit (38 °Celsius). Due to the high temperatures and dry air, fires and drought are a near constant hazard.

Mediterranean Chaparral

The Mediterranean chaparral follows this general pattern of high temperatures and minimal precipitation. Much of this area's moisture comes in the form of fog from the oceans nearby. Rain, however, does fall. During winter, the Mediterranean chaparral receives about 7 inches

Eco Facts

In chaparrals, the rainy season peaks in February. Precipitation slows down after February and completely stops in May.

Thunderstorms occur often in chaparral ecosystems. Fire is a risk, as lightning sometimes strikes.

(17.5 cm) of rain. Spring brings about 2 inches (5 cm) of rain. Less than 1 inch (2.5 cm) is received in summer, and about 4 inches (10 cm) of rain falls in the region during the autumn months.

California Chaparral

The climate in the California chaparral ecosystem is much like the Mediterranean region. However, the higher altitudes of the California mountains are cooler and receive more precipitation than the lower regions of this ecosystem. In fact, at its highest points, the California chaparral sometimes experiences freezing temperatures. This does not last long, and any snow that falls melts quickly. Most of the moisture in this area comes in the form of rain, with the region receiving 12 to 40 inches (30 to 102 cm) annually. The rainfall is evenly distributed among the autumn, winter, and spring seasons.

California Chaparral Climatogram

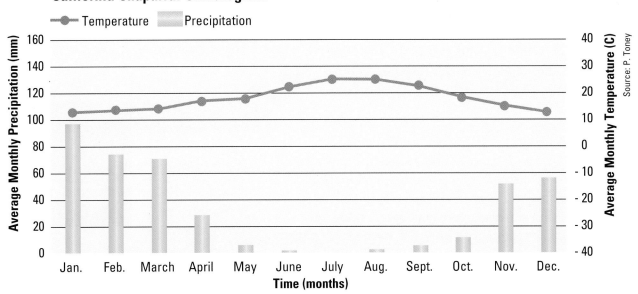

Source: P. Toney

Chaparral Features

Clanwilliam cedar is one of the largest trees in the African fynbos. It can grow up to 65 feet (20 m) tall.

Most chaparral ecosystems formed as a result of human activity. These areas were once covered with forests. As human populations spread, the land was needed for other purposes. The forests were cut down to make room for farm animals to graze. Over time, this grazing caused the soil to lose many of its **nutrients**. The forests could not grow again because of the damaged soil. The soil became vulnerable to **erosion** by wind and rain. Erosion removed even more nutrients from the area, making it difficult for the soil to become fertile again. Only thick, tough vegetation can grow in these conditions. The chaparral plants overtook the land. As a result, the chaparral is known for its nutrient-poor soil and shrublike plant life.

The plant life of the chaparral can be divided into two groups. Hard, or true, chaparral is normally found in dry, inland areas that receive little precipitation, including fog. Soft chaparral is usually found in fog belt areas, but can also develop in areas where hard chaparral has experienced fire. In these instances, the soft chaparral is a temporary growth and is replaced by hard chaparral over time.

Eco Facts

The oils in many soft chaparral plants are heavily scented. This repels animals that might otherwise feed on them.

The roots of some hard chaparral plants extend as far as 30 feet (9 m) into the ground.

Types of Chaparral

The location of a chaparral often determines the type of plant growth that occurs in the ecosystem.

Maquis Chaparral

Also known as the chamiso-redshank, the maquis is the most common type of chaparral. Found in both Europe and California, this type of chaparral contains both large and small shrubs as well as a variety of small plants. All of this **vegetation** is packed tightly together in a dense mass.

Garigue Chaparral

Garigue chaparral is found mainly in Europe. In these areas, the soil is so poor in nutrients that large shrubs cannot grow. Instead, this chaparral is characterized by the growth of **herbs** and small shrubs. This type of chaparral often moves into areas of maquis chaparral that human development has destroyed.

Coastal Scrub Chaparral

Coastal scrub chaparral is found in the coastal areas of California. It tends to grow in areas that have been destroyed by humans. Coastal scrub chaparral often consists of soft chaparral plants.

Mixed Chaparral

Mixed chaparral is found in California. Located on mountainsides with elevations up to 5,500 feet (1,676 meters), mixed chaparral contains shrubs and trees that grow to a height of about 15 feet (5 m).

Montane Chaparral

Montane chaparral is found on the mountains of California. In montane chaparral, large shrubs and dwarf trees grow at elevations up to 9,000 feet (2,743 m). These trees and shrubs rarely grow taller than 10 feet (3 m).

Chaparral ecosystems are the natural habitat of many different plants and animals. The plants and animals that survive in these areas have adapted to the conditions. They are able to live in very dry areas by conserving as much water as possible.

Producers

The plants found in chaparrals act as producers for other organisms in the ecosystem. These organisms are called producers because they make their own food. They also serve as food for other organisms. Producers absorb energy from the Sun and convert it into usable forms of energy such as sugar. They make this energy through a process called **photosynthesis**. Producers found in chaparrals include many types of grass and shrubs, such as sagebrush.

Primary Consumers

The insects and animals that rely on producers as a food source are called primary consumers. When a primary consumer feeds on a producer, the energy made by the producer is transferred to the consumer. Examples of primary consumers found in chaparral ecosystems include insects, such as stink beetles and butterflies, and small mammals, including jackrabbits and kangaroo rats.

Chaparral Energy Pyramid

The transfer of energy in an ecosystem begins with producers and moves up the energy pyramid to the tertiary consumers. Organisms at each level of the pyramid receive energy from the organisms in the level below them.

Outside of the pyramid are the decomposers. They break down the dead and decaying **organic** matter left behind when plants and animals die. For this reason, decomposers receive energy from organisms in all levels of the energy pyramid.

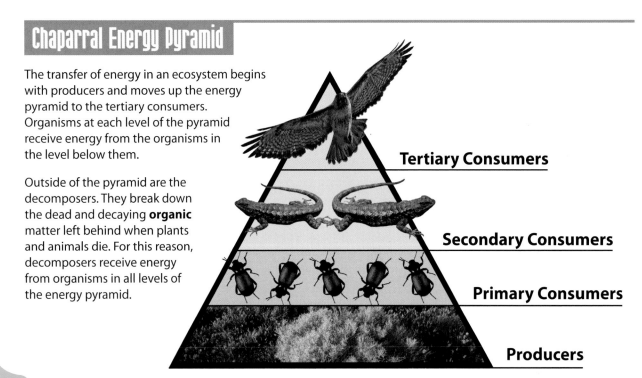

Tertiary Consumers

Secondary Consumers

Primary Consumers

Producers

Chaparral Food Web

Another way to study the flow of energy through an ecosystem is by examining food chains and food webs. A food chain shows how a producer feeds a primary consumer, which then feeds a secondary consumer, and so on. However, most organisms feed on many different food sources. This practice causes food chains to interconnect, creating a food web.

In this example, the **red line** represents one food chain from the grass, jackrabbit, and coyote. The blue line from the sagebrush, stink beetle, ground squirrel, and coyote form another food chain. These food chains connect at the coyote, but they also connect in other places. The jackrabbit also feeds from sagebrush, and the stink beetle also eats grass. This series of connections forms a complex food web.

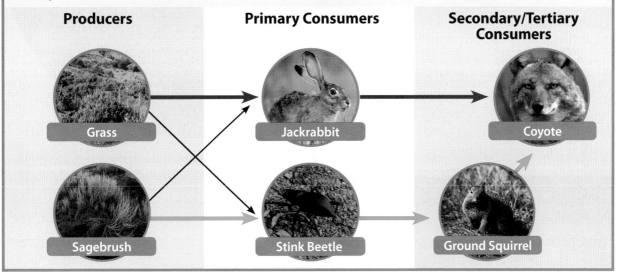

Producers	**Primary Consumers**	**Secondary/Tertiary Consumers**
Grass	Jackrabbit	Coyote
Sagebrush	Stink Beetle	Ground Squirrel

Secondary and Tertiary Consumers

Secondary consumers feed on both producers and primary consumers. In the chaparral, secondary consumers include reptiles and **amphibians**, such as whiptail lizards and some kinds of newts. Mammals such as ground squirrels are also secondary consumers. Larger carnivores, including coyotes, and some large snakes, such as rattlesnakes, are called tertiary consumers. Tertiary consumers feed on secondary consumers.

Decomposers

Fungi, such as mushrooms and mold, and many types of bacteria live in chaparral ecosystems. These organisms are called decomposers because they eat dead and decaying organic materials. Decomposers speed up the process of breaking down dead organic materials and releasing their nutrients into the soil. These nutrients are then absorbed by the roots of shrubs and other plants.

Plants

Shrubs

Vegetation in the chaparral ecosystem is mainly composed of different shrub species. These plants have adapted to living with the fires, heat, and dryness of the region. Two of the most common shrubs found in chaparrals are the chamise and the manzanita. The chamise is an evergreen shrub that grows to between 3 and 10 feet (1 and 3 m) in height. Chamise can be used to make tea and was used by American Indians and settlers to treat diseases, such as tetanus and rabies. Manzanita is often found in montane chaparral. The word *manzanita* means "little apple" in Spanish. The plant was given this name because of its small red and green fruit.

The king protea is the national flower of South Africa, where it thrives in the fynbos.

Cactus

Beavertail cactus and Lee pincushion cactus are two species of cactus that grow in the California chaparral. The stems of the beavertail are flat and paddlelike, resembling the tail of a beaver. They are blue-green in color for most of the year, but sometimes turn deep purple with the approach of winter. Beavertail cactus blooms in the spring with flowers that are deep rose. Lee pincushion cactus grows in interior chaparral regions. It is normally found growing in small cracks in the ground.

The pink fruit of the prickly pear cactus is thought to have medicinal uses.

Herbs

Oregano, sage, rosemary, and thyme are a few of the herbs that grow in the chaparral regions of the world. Oregano is an herb that originated in the Mediterranean. It is a common ingredient in Greek and Italian cooking. Oregano is a member of the mint family of plants. The word *oregano* means "joy of the mountains." Sage plants grow to about 3 feet (1 m) in height. This herb is commonly used to season turkey and other meats. As a tea, it can also be used to fight illness, such as a cold. Rosemary grows wild in the Mediterranean region. Like oregano and sage, this herb is used in cooking. Rosemary is thought to have medicinal uses. Some people use it to relieve aching joints. Thyme is another herb native to the Mediterranean region. It has a lemon flavor and is often used in French cooking. Like sage, it is used to ward off a cold.

Oregano has a strong aroma and a slightly bitter taste.

Birds and Mammals

Cactus Wrens

More than 100 kinds of bird live in the chaparral region of California. Living in this hot region has forced these birds to adapt to the heat. One of the most common birds in the California chaparral is the cactus wren. It is a small bird—only about 9 inches (22 cm) long. However, it is the largest wren in the United States. This curious bird is as active as it is eye-catching. It is not very colorful, but the white on its throat, belly, and sides is a startling contrast to its spotted breast. Some other birds that live in chaparrals include the rock dove, house sparrow, yellow-billed cuckoo, rough-winged swallow, and black-chinned hummingbird.

The cactus wren has adapted to survive without freestanding water from rivers or lakes.

California Quails

The California quail is California's state bird. It is a favorite of birdwatchers and hunters. The quail makes its nest in brushy or grassy places. The quail is a monogamous bird. This means that it has only one mate during the breeding season.

Instead of drinking, the California quail receives most of its water through the food it eats.

Bezoar Goats

Like birds, some mammals have adapted to the harsh environment of chaparral ecosystems. The Bezoar goat is commonly referred

to as the wild goat. It can be found on many Greek islands, as well as in Turkey, Pakistan, and Iran. The Bezoar goat can weigh up to 300 pounds (136 kilograms), but this weight is often hidden by the thick wool that covers its body. The most common colors for the Bezoar goat are white, gray, brown, red, and black. The horns of Bezoar goats grow in the shape of a scimitar, which is a curved and deadly sword.

Gray Foxes

The gray fox is commonly known as the tree fox. It lives in the southwestern United States and can be found in the California chaparral. The gray fox prefers to live in wooded areas that are covered with bushes. It is a **nocturnal** animal, so it sleeps during the day and hunts at night. Being an **omnivore**, the gray fox eats nuts and berries and also hunts small animals, such as rats and rabbits. A gray fox can live for about 12 years in captivity, but its lifespan in the hot, dry chaparral is much shorter.

Coyotes can be found throughout North America, including the California chaparral, where they feed on anything from rabbits and rodents to insects and grass.

Insects, Reptiles, and Amphibians

Insects

Many different kinds of insects can be found in chaparral ecosystems. Flies, honeybees, and ladybugs flit about chaparrals. Cockroaches make their home under rocks. Butterflies and moths **pollinate** the hardy flowers of the chaparral. Some of the most common insects found in chaparral ecosystems are butterflies, moths, cockroaches, beetles, flies, and midges. One of the largest flying insects in the chaparral region is the sphinx moth, which can have wingspan of more than 5 inches (12.5 cm). The western wood cockroach resides in or under the logs and rocks of the chaparral. It feeds on decaying plant matter found in the area.

The size and rapid wing movement of the sphinx moth have led some people to call it a hummingbird moth.

Reptiles

Many reptiles make their home in chaparral ecosystems. Reptiles help maintain insect populations in the ecosystem while providing a food source for larger **predators**. Some of the reptiles that can be found in chaparral ecosystems include rattlesnakes, gopher snakes, western fence lizards, and side-blotched lizards. Reptiles are often difficult to spot in chaparral ecosystems because many are nocturnal. Others have adapted to be inactive during the times when humans are most likely to be around.

California is home to seven species of rattlesnake, which can be found in both the desert and the chaparral.

Eco Facts

When a stink beetle is picked up, it releases a foul-smelling, reddish-black liquid. This is how the beetle received its name.

The yucca moth is the only insect that pollinates yucca plants. It does this by stuffing a small ball of **pollen** into the center of each flower.

Amphibians

Although chaparrals are generally too hot and dry for amphibians, these animals are still sometimes found in these ecosystems. Amphibians most often occur in areas where chaparral ecosystems border forests or watered canyons. Some species of salamanders and toads will venture into chaparrals during temperate winter or spring nights, especially during rain. Amphibians usually move to cool, moist areas during the hotter times of year.

The California newt is often found in chaparral ecosystems. This amphibian can release a powerful venom when threatened. One drop of this venom can kill 7,000 mice.

Chaparrals in Danger

Chaparral ecosystems are under constant threat of fire. Every 30 to 40 years, chaparrals experience natural fires that destroy large areas of land and the nutrients they contain. Fire is a necessity to these ecosystems. It rids the area of dense plant growth that has been on the land for years. This allows new growth to emerge. In this way, fires allow chaparrals to regenerate.

Natural fires, however, can quickly become uncontrollable. Chaparral plants are dry and burn quickly, allowing the fire to spread a great distance in a short amount of time. Fires in chaparrals have been known to move at a rate of 8 miles (13 km) per hour. These fires quickly consume everything in their path.

While fire is good for chaparrals in many ways, it also has an adverse effect on the ecosystem. Plants that have been growing in the chaparral for long periods of time become rooted firmly in the soil. These plants and roots help hold the soil in place. When fire destroys the dense plant growth, the barrier that was protecting the soil is removed. The soil and nutrients can be shifted easily and washed away. This makes the ground water-resistant. Since the water does not soak in, the soil remains very dry.

Timeline of Human Activity in Chaparrals

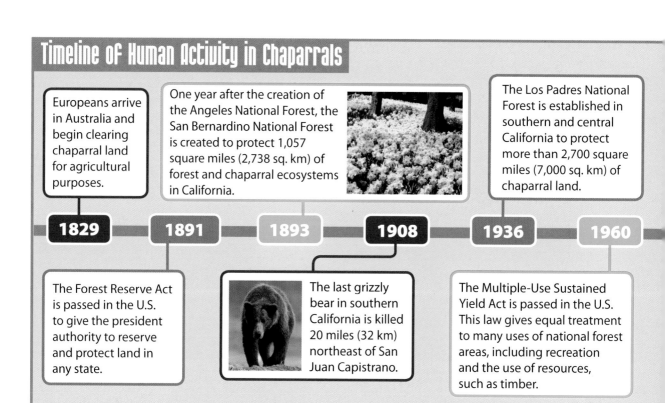

Europeans arrive in Australia and begin clearing chaparral land for agricultural purposes.

One year after the creation of the Angeles National Forest, the San Bernardino National Forest is created to protect 1,057 square miles (2,738 sq. km) of forest and chaparral ecosystems in California.

The Los Padres National Forest is established in southern and central California to protect more than 2,700 square miles (7,000 sq. km) of chaparral land.

1829 · **1891** · **1893** · **1908** · **1936** · **1960**

The Forest Reserve Act is passed in the U.S. to give the president authority to reserve and protect land in any state.

The last grizzly bear in southern California is killed 20 miles (32 km) northeast of San Juan Capistrano.

The Multiple-Use Sustained Yield Act is passed in the U.S. This law gives equal treatment to many uses of national forest areas, including recreation and the use of resources, such as timber.

To keep the problem under control, some governments are letting people start fires in small parcels of land. This process is called controlled burning. It reduces the risk of the fire spreading into farmland and other nearby residential areas. The California Department of Forestry has allowed ranchers to start controlled fires in the California chaparral for almost 50 years. Still, as much as controlled burning helps stop massive fires, they do still occur. It is difficult to predict when and where a fire will break out in chaparral ecosystems. Fires will continue to occur in chaparrals on a regular basis.

Firefighters are often called upon to help control the spread of wildfires in chaparral ecosystems through controlled burns.

A report from the Royal Swedish Academy of Sciences finds that overpopulation and deforestation for agricultural purposes has destroyed much of the Mediterranean chaparral ecosystem.

A study finds that the Chilean chaparral supports 53 percent of the country's population, 50 percent of the total plant species in the area, and 45 percent of plant species found only in this ecosystem.

There are now more than 300 million people living in the Mediterranean Basin, home of the maquis, or chaparral, ecosystems. A shortage of water and **desertification** are becoming a threat to **biodiversity** in the area.

1965   **1974**   **1995**   **1998**   **2007**   **2012**

Root disease is first identified in southwestern Australia. The fungal disease later spreads to infest thousands of acres (hectares) of chaparral and forest areas.

Table Mountain National Park is created in South Africa, becoming one of the largest protected areas for Africa fynbos.

A wildfire burns through the southern California chaparral, scorching an area of about 770 square miles (1,994 sq. km). More than 1,780 homes are destroyed in the blaze.

Science in the Chaparral

Satellites are often used to monitor weather conditions in the California chaparral.

Chaparral ecosystems face unique challenges to their survival. Due to their poor soil, only certain types of plants can grow in these areas. Yet, even these plants are in danger of disappearing due to air pollution, fire, drought, and human activities. Scientists constantly study chaparral regions to assess the dangers that threaten the ecosystem. Global Positioning System/Global Information System (GPS/GIS) technologies, remote sensing, and **automated** field mapping techniques are just a few of the methods used to track the vegetation of the chaparral.

Tracking Growth in the Chaparral

GPS and GIS are both used to monitor plant growth in the chaparral. GPS locates where the plants are growing in the ecosystem. GIS tracks which plants are growing where. By knowing where certain plants are growing, scientists can analyze the area to determine the conditions needed to grow these plants. It can also help scientists understand why other plants do not grow in the area. GPS also alerts scientists to the disappearance of some plants from an area. The scientists can then study the factors that led to the disappearance and suggest solutions to improve the environment so the plants can grow again.

Remote Sensing

Remote sensing also helps scientists track plant growth in the chaparral. Like GPS, remote sensing uses satellites to locate plants. In remote sensing, the satellites provide **infrared** images that show scientists the plants growing in an area, as well as all of the other objects found in the area. This is another tool that helps scientists assess the conditions under which certain plants grow. It also helps determine how changes to the environment, including pollution and temperature changes, affect plant growth.

Eco Facts

GIS has a variety of uses, including emergency planning. By tracking emergency calls and travel times, the system can be used to calculate response times during disasters and other crises, including chaparral fires.

Mapping the Chaparral

To properly understand the information obtained from GPS/GIS and remote sensing, scientists must have a place to put it when it is gathered. Computer-automated field mapping programs have been developed for this purpose. They allow scientists to create a picture of a chaparral ecosystem. Scientists can see which plants grow in the ecosystem, where these plants are growing, and what other plants, animals, and objects share the ecosystem with them. They can also map the conditions affecting the ecosystem, including air quality and human development. By putting all of the information together, the scientists can properly assess and address the issues facing the ecosystem.

Aside from scientists, GPS is now also used by other people in chaparral ecosystems, such as hikers and outdoor enthusiasts.

Working in the Chaparral

Biologists, botanists, and ecologists often work in chaparrals, studying the plants and animals that live in the ecosystem.

Chaparral ecosystems are one of the most heavily studied ecosystems in the world. The fires, nutrients, climate, and everyday happenings in chaparral ecosystems are of great importance to ecologists, climatologists, and soil scientists.

Ecologist

Duties

Studies the relationship between organisms and their environment

Education

Bachelor's, master's, or doctoral degree in science

Interests

Biology and statistics

A love of nature is essential for an ecologist. Ecologists spend much of their time outdoors studying the natural world. They study the relationships between plants and animals to understand how ecosystems work. Ecologists study the life cycles of plants and animals, keeping track of the number and types of plants and animals that live in a certain area.

Other Chaparral Jobs

Climatologist

Analyzes and forecasts long-term weather patterns, and conducts research into processes and phenomena of weather, climate, and the atmosphere

Soil Scientist

Studies different types of soil and the implications of soil use

Biologist

Studies the plant and animal life found in chaparrals and anything that affects the natural balance in the ecosystem

David Brower

David Ross Brower (1912–2000) was a distinguished ecologist and an active environmentalist. Most of his work was done in the mountain and chaparral regions of California. Brower wrote four books, including *Only a Little Planet* (1975), *For Earth's Sake: The Life and Times of David Brower* (1990), and *Let the Mountains Talk, Let the Rivers Run* (1995).

Born in Berkeley, California, Brower began his lifelong campaign of environmental activism when he joined the Sierra Club in 1933. By 1952, he had become the Sierra Club's first executive director. After leaving the club in 1969, Brower formed the conservation group Friends of the Earth (FOE) to raise awareness of acid rain, global warming, and pollution. In 1982, he started the Earth Island Institute to promote and develop environmental conservation projects around the world.

Brower's work in environmental conservation earned him international fame. He successfully fought against the construction of dams at Dinosaur National Monument and in Grand Canyon National Park. He also led campaigns that established 10 national parks and seashores. The passing of the Wilderness Act of 1964 is another of Brower's success stories. This law protects millions of acres (hectares) of land. Brower was nominated for the Nobel Peace Prize three times, in 1978, 1979, and 1998.

Watering Soil

Soil in chaparral ecosystems is very dry and holds few nutrients. The ability of soil to hold moisture is affected by its composition. When a plant is unable to hold moisture, its ability to support plant life is affected. Try this activity to see how water passes through different types of soil.

Materials

3 Soil Samples **3 Jars** **3 Coffee Filters** **3 Funnels**

A Pen **Paper** **Stopwatch or Timer** **Water**

1. Put each soil sample in a jar, and label each jar.

2. Place a coffee filter inside each funnel, and place the funnels into the jars.

3. Pour 1/2 cup (125 milliliters) of each soil sample onto a piece of paper. Weigh each sample. On another piece of paper, create a chart to note the weights.

4. Pour the soil samples into the separate funnels. Set the timer for 30 minutes. Pour 1/2 cup (125 ml) of water into each funnel.

5. Watch to see when the water starts to drip through the filter. On your chart, record how long it took for the water to begin dripping from each sample.

6. After 30 minutes, remove the funnels, and measure the volume of water that has drained from the sample into the jar. Note the amounts on your chart.

7. Empty each soil sample onto a fresh piece of paper, and weigh it again. Record the weights on your chart.

Results

Which samples absorbed and held water the best? Why do you think this happened?

Create a Food Web

U se this book, and research on the Internet, to create a food web of chaparral ecosystem plants and animals. Start by finding at least three organisms of each type—producers, primary consumers, secondary consumers, and tertiary consumers. Then, begin linking these organisms together into food chains. Draw the arrows of each food chain in a different color. Use a **red** pen or crayon for one food chain and green and blue for the others. You should find that many of these food chains connect, creating a food web. Add the rest of the arrows to complete the food web using a pencil or **black** pen.

Once your food web is complete, use it to answer the following questions.

1 How would removing one organism from your food web affect the other organisms in the web?

2 What would happen to the rest of the food web if the producers were taken away?

3 How would decomposers fit into the food web?

Sample Food Web

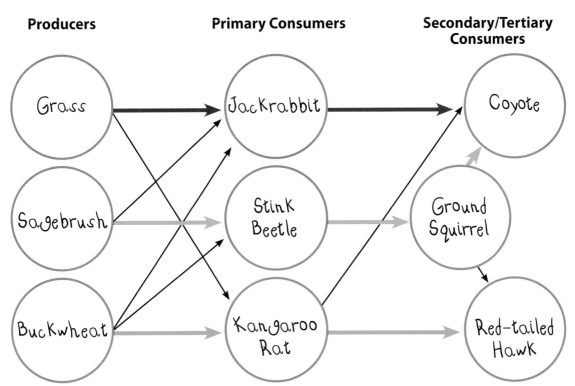

Eco Challenge

1. On what part of a continent are chaparral ecosystems normally found?

2. What are the latitude coordinates for the major locations of chaparral ecosystems around the world?

3. How hot does the chaparral ecosystem usually get in the summer?

4. How often do major fires sweep through chaparral ecosystems?

5. At what rate of speed does fire travel in a chaparral ecosystem?

6. How many different kinds of birds live in the California chaparral?

7. What is another name for chamise? Why is it called this?

8. What technologies are used to study chaparrals?

9. What do ecologists study?

10. How much rain does a chaparral ecosystem usually get in a year?

Answers

1. On the western part of continents
2. Between 30° and 40° latitude
3. Up to 100°F (38°C)
4. Every 30 to 40 years
5. At a rate of 8 miles (13 km) per hour
6. More than 100 different kinds of birds
7. Greasewood; because it burns quickly and intensely, like grease
8. GPS/GIS, remote sensing, automated mapping
9. Ecologists study the relationship between organisms and the environment in which they live
10. Between 10 and 17 inches (25 and 42 cm)

Glossary

amphibians: cold-blooded animals with moist, smooth skin

automated: a machine that does a job that used to be done by people

biodiversity: the variety of plant and animal life in an ecosystem

biome: a large area where certain kinds of plants and animals can be found; can include more than one ecosystem

desertification: the process through which fertile land turns into desert

ecosystem: a community of living things sharing an environment

endemic: native to a particular area

erosion: the process of wearing away by wind, rain, and glaciers

herbs: plants whose leaves, stems, seeds, or roots are used in cooking or medicines

infrared: a type of light that is not visible to the human eye

nocturnal: active at night

nutrients: substances that feed plants or animals

omnivore: an animal that eats plants and other animals

organic: made up of living things

organisms: living things

photosynthesis: the process in which a green plant uses sunlight to change water and carbon dioxide into food for itself

pollen: a yellow powder made in flowers

pollinate: to transfer pollen from one plant to another to fertilize it

predators: animals that hunt other animals for food

species: a group of similar animals that can mate together

vegetation: plant life

Index

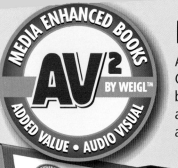

Log on to www.av2books.com

AV² by Weigl brings you media enhanced books that support active learning. Go to www.av2books.com, and enter the special code found on page 2 of this book. You will gain access to enriched and enhanced content that supplements and complements this book. Content includes video, audio, weblinks, quizzes, a slide show, and activities.

Audio
Listen to sections of
the book read aloud.

Video
Watch informative video clips.

Embedded Weblinks
Gain additional information
for research.

Try This!
Complete activities and
hands-on experiments.

WHAT'S ONLINE?

Try This!	Embedded Weblinks	Video	EXTRA FEATURES
Complete an activity to test your knowledge of the levels of organization in a chaparral ecosystem.	Find out more information on chaparral ecosystems.	Watch a video about chaparral ecosystems.	**Audio** Listen to sections of the book read aloud.
Complete an activity to test your knowledge of energy pyramids.	Learn more about the animals that live in chaparral ecosystems.	Watch a video about animals that live in chaparral ecosystems.	**Key Words** Study vocabulary, and complete a matching word activity.
Create a timeline of important events in chaparral ecosystems.	Find out more about the plants that grow in chaparral ecosystems.		**Slide Show** View images and captions, and prepare a presentation.
Write a biography about a scientist.	Read about current research in chaparral ecosystems.		**Quizzes** Test your knowledge.
	Learn more about threats facing chaparral ecosystems.		

AV² was built to bridge the gap between print and digital. We encourage you to tell us what you like and what you want to see in the future.
Sign up to be an AV² Ambassador at www.av2books.com/ambassador.